Playful

KOREAN

Food

Coloring Book

SEOUL
Sweets
THE SWEETEST BOOKS YOU'VE EVER READ

ILLUSTRATED & WRITTEN
BY ANA CHOI

Korean Street Food Fun!
Korean streets are full of tasty snacks like fish cakes, tteokbokki, corn dogs, and hotteok. These treats are cheap, delicious, and clean—perfect for a quick bite. Let's explore the vibrant world of Korean street food!

Bungeobbang Ice Cream: A Sweet Catch!
Bungeobbang, a fish-shaped cake, is a favorite Korean snack. Today, it's even filled with ice cream and decorated with chocolate sticks or treats for extra fun and flavor!

Bingsu: A Cool Summer Treat!
Bingsu, or shaved ice, is a popular summer dessert in Korea. The classic version is topped with sweet red beans and rice cakes, but you can add ice cream, fresh fruits, or any toppings you like for extra fun!

Tteok: A Colorful Korean Treat!

Tteok, or rice cake, is a traditional Korean dessert enjoyed for generations. Like bakeries, tteok shops are found in every town, offering a variety of colorful and uniquely shaped rice cakes. Let your imagination shine as you color them!

Gimbap: A Picnic Favorite!

Gimbap is a must-have for Korean picnics, school field trips, or days by the river or mountains. These tasty seaweed rice rolls are the perfect food to pack for a fun and exciting day!

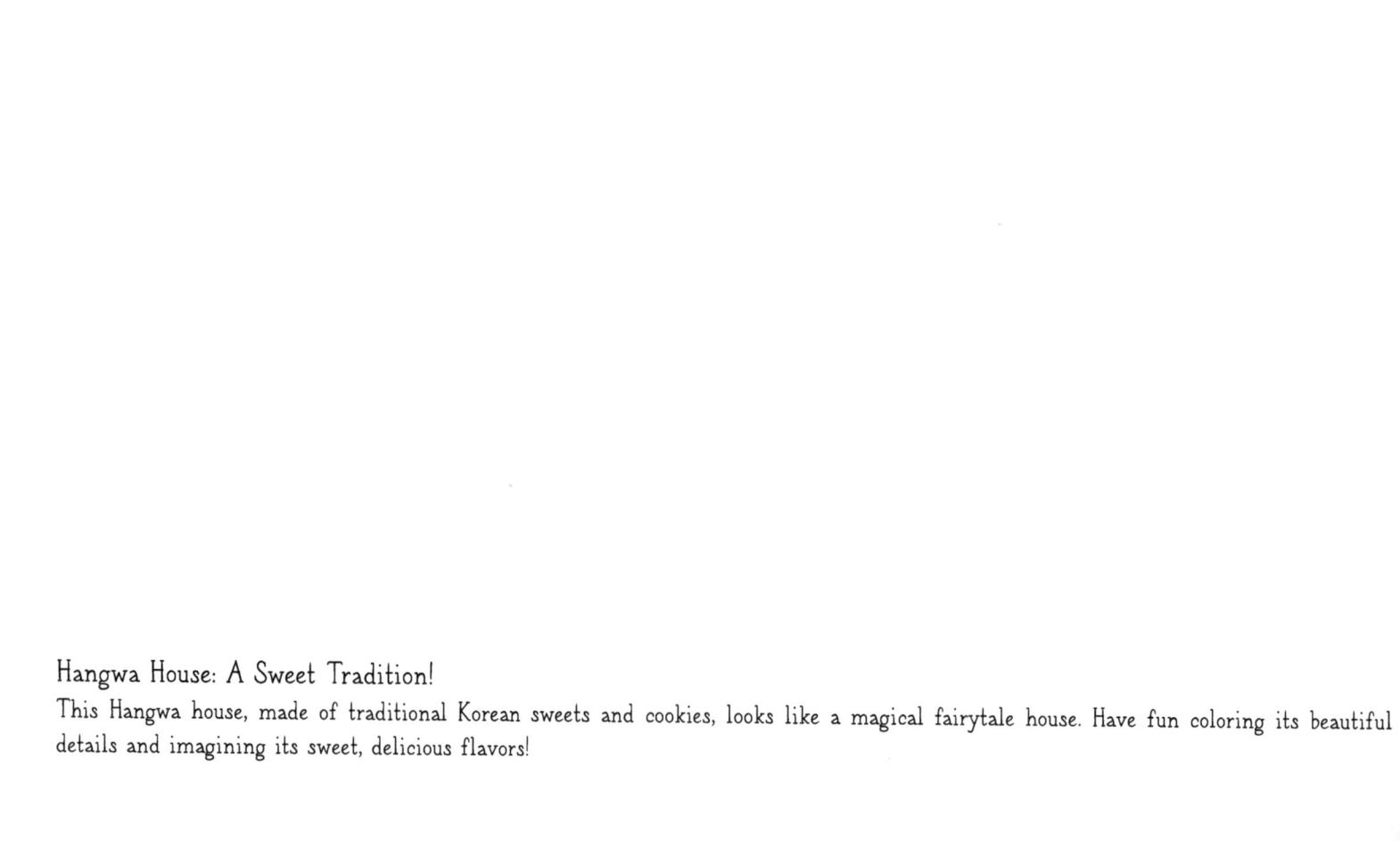

Hangwa House: A Sweet Tradition!
This Hangwa house, made of traditional Korean sweets and cookies, looks like a magical fairytale house. Have fun coloring its beautiful details and imagining its sweet, delicious flavors!

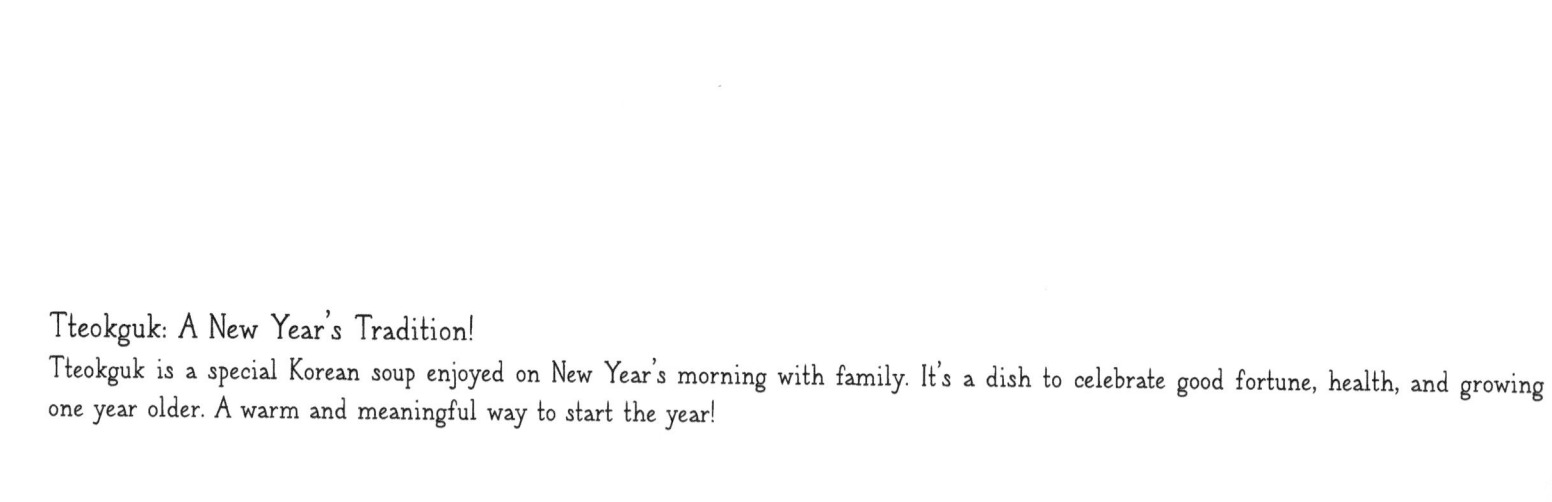

Tteokguk: A New Year's Tradition!

Tteokguk is a special Korean soup enjoyed on New Year's morning with family. It's a dish to celebrate good fortune, health, and growing one year older. A warm and meaningful way to start the year!

Jipbap: A Traditional Korean Homemade Meal

Jipbap, a typical Korean homemade meal, includes a bowl of steamed rice, a main dish like fish or meat, and three small side dishes called banchan. A hearty jjigae (stew) or guk (soup) always accompanies the meal, and of course, kimchi is a must on the table!

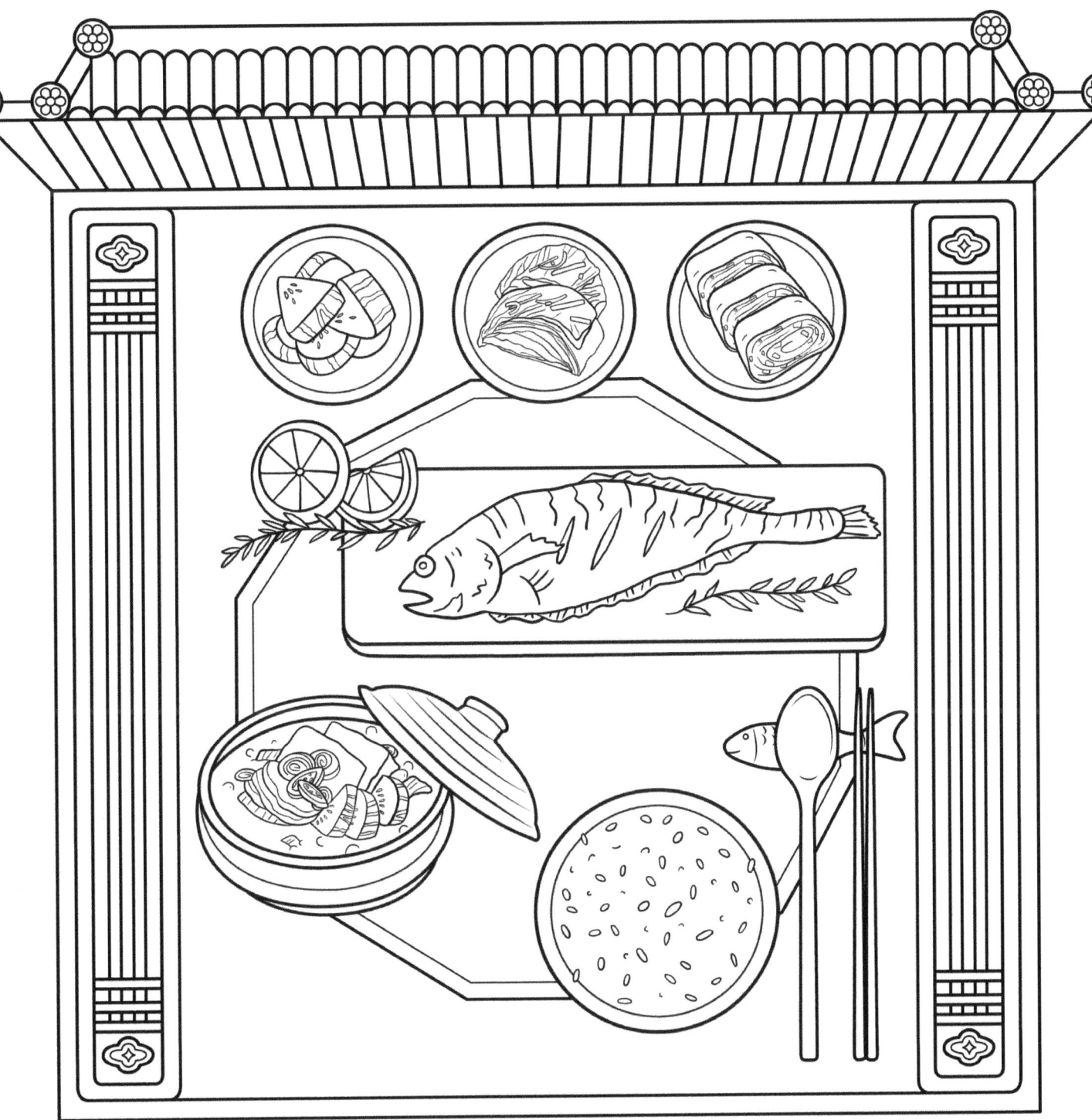

Bbeongtuigi: A Puffed Snack Fun!
Bbeongtuigi is puffed rice or corn, made by popping it in a traditional puffing machine. When it bursts out, it looks like popcorn snow! These light, crunchy snacks come in fun shapes and colors, loved by kids and adults alike.

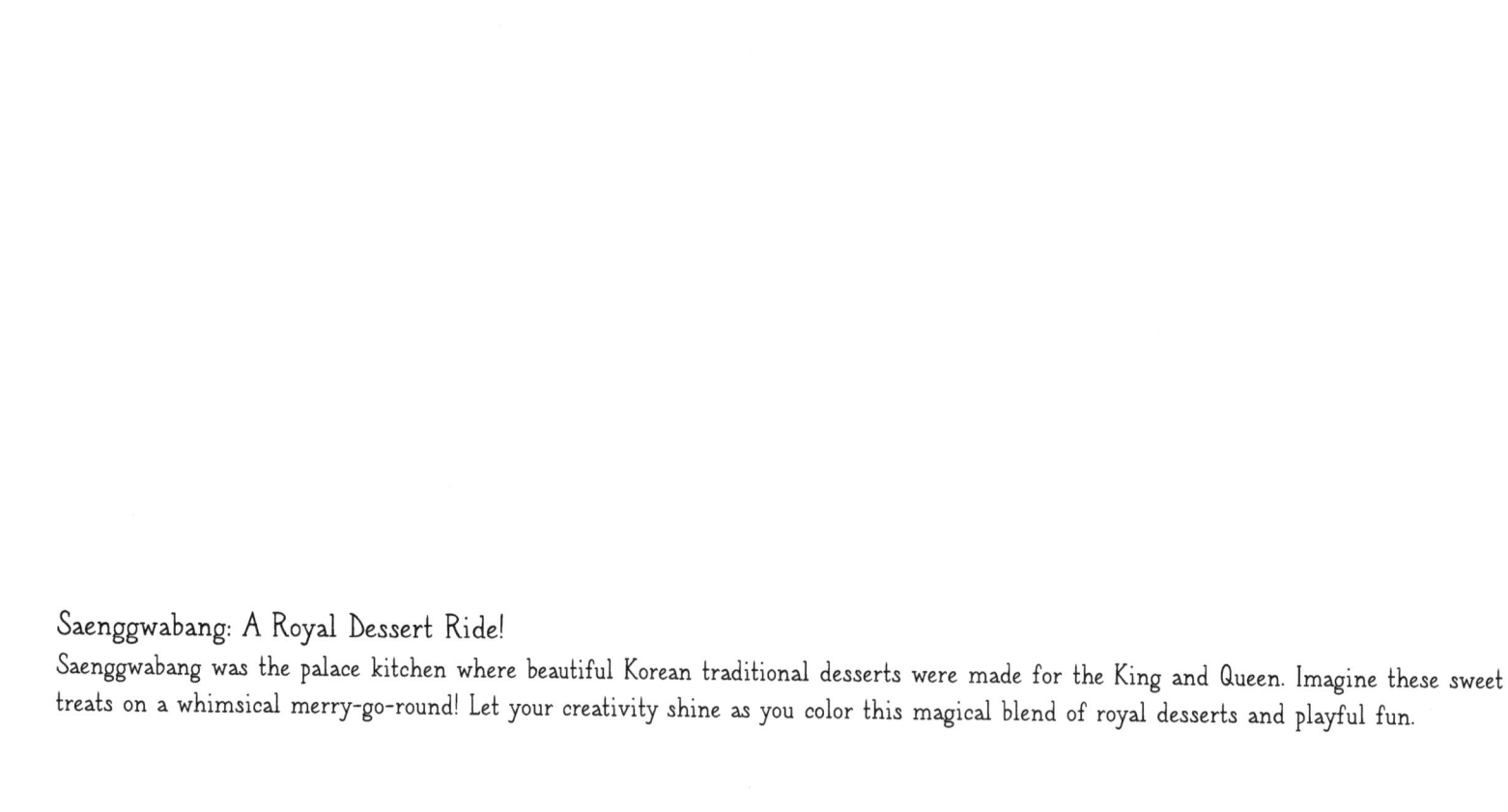

Saenggwabang: A Royal Dessert Ride!

Saenggwabang was the palace kitchen where beautiful Korean traditional desserts were made for the King and Queen. Imagine these sweet treats on a whimsical merry-go-round! Let your creativity shine as you color this magical blend of royal desserts and playful fun.

Subak Hwachae: A Summer Treat!
Subak Hwachae, or watermelon punch, is the perfect way to cool off on a hot summer day. Add your favorite fruits and drinks, and dive into this refreshing watermelon pool!

Gimbap: A Colorful Roll!
These days, Gimbap comes in many varieties like tuna, vegetable, and egg. Have fun coloring the different kinds of colorful and tasty Gimbap rolls!

Jeon: A Festive Fritter!
Jeon, Korean fritters, are a tasty treat for celebrations. They're colorful, simple, and smell so good you'll want to try them right away!

Cup Ramyun: A Quick and Tasty Treat!

Cup noodles are a quick and delicious meal in Korea. With so many flavors to choose from, you can enjoy this easy snack just the way you like it!

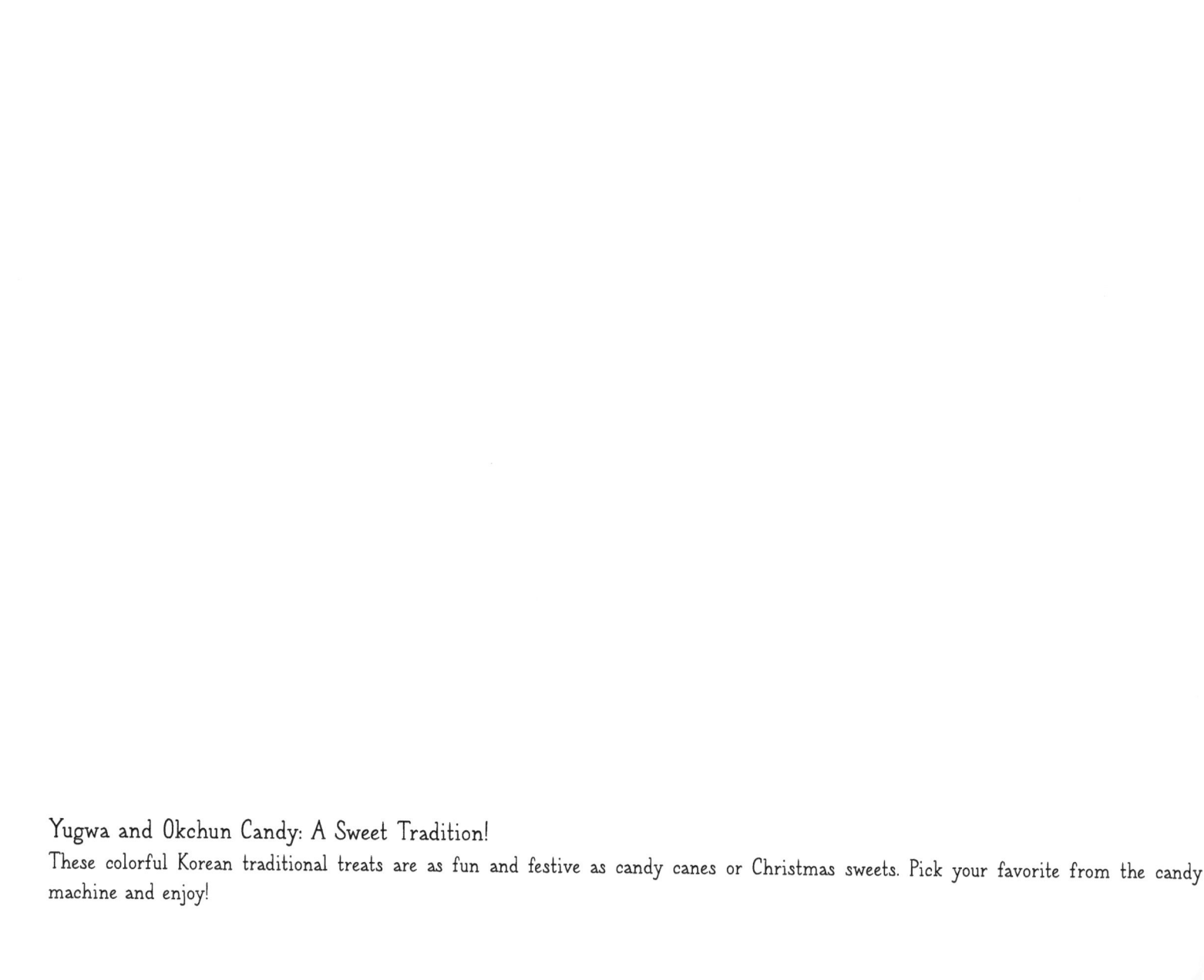

Yugwa and Okchun Candy: A Sweet Tradition!
These colorful Korean traditional treats are as fun and festive as candy canes or Christmas sweets. Pick your favorite from the candy machine and enjoy!

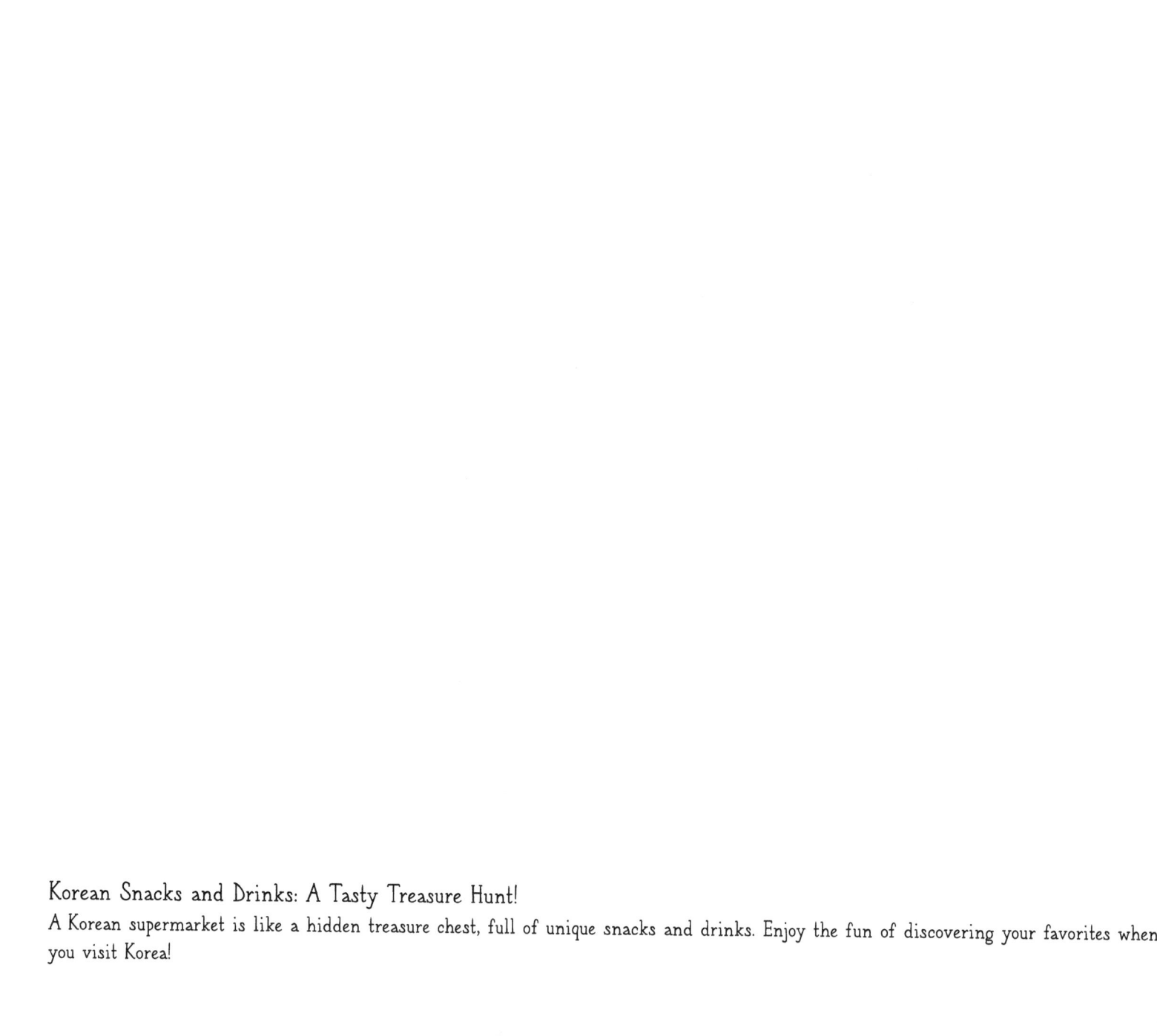

Korean Snacks and Drinks: A Tasty Treasure Hunt!
A Korean supermarket is like a hidden treasure chest, full of unique snacks and drinks. Enjoy the fun of discovering your favorites when you visit Korea!

Gungoguma: A Winter Favorite!
Baked sweet potatoes are one of Korea's favorite winter snacks. During chilly winters, you'll find baking machines on the streets, filling the air with a warm, sweet aroma. Korean sweet potatoes are extra sweet because they grow in Korea's colder regions!

Boseong Nokcha Village: The Home of Green Tea!
Boseong is Korea's famous region for green tea, with beautiful, sprawling tea farms. Here, you can enjoy not only fresh green tea but also tasty green tea treats like ice cream, rice cakes, lattes, and cakes!

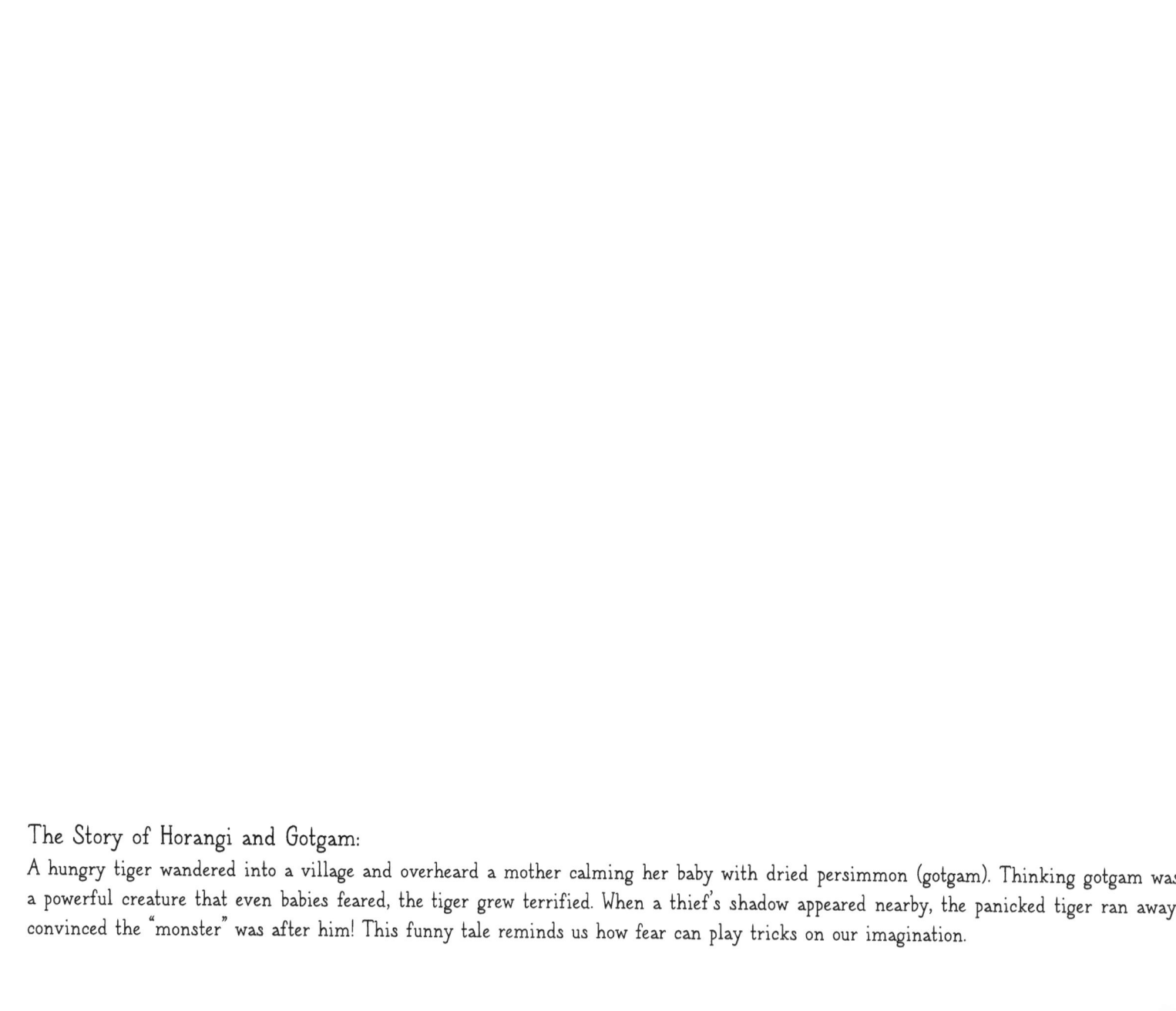

The Story of Horangi and Gotgam:
A hungry tiger wandered into a village and overheard a mother calming her baby with dried persimmon (gotgam). Thinking gotgam was a powerful creature that even babies feared, the tiger grew terrified. When a thief's shadow appeared nearby, the panicked tiger ran away, convinced the "monster" was after him! This funny tale reminds us how fear can play tricks on our imagination.

Ttalgi: Sweet Korean Strawberries!
Korean strawberries are extra sweet and delicious, especially in March when they're in season. Strawberry festivals pop up across Korea, offering tasty strawberry desserts and treats for everyone to enjoy!

STRAWBERRY FESTIVAL

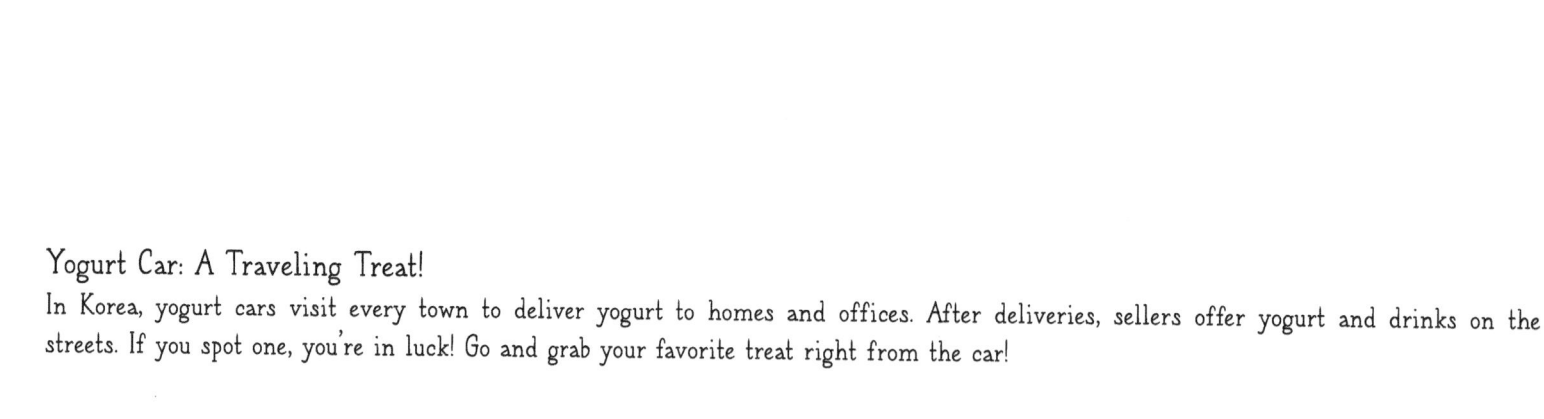

Yogurt Car: A Traveling Treat!
In Korea, yogurt cars visit every town to deliver yogurt to homes and offices. After deliveries, sellers offer yogurt and drinks on the streets. If you spot one, you're in luck! Go and grab your favorite treat right from the car!

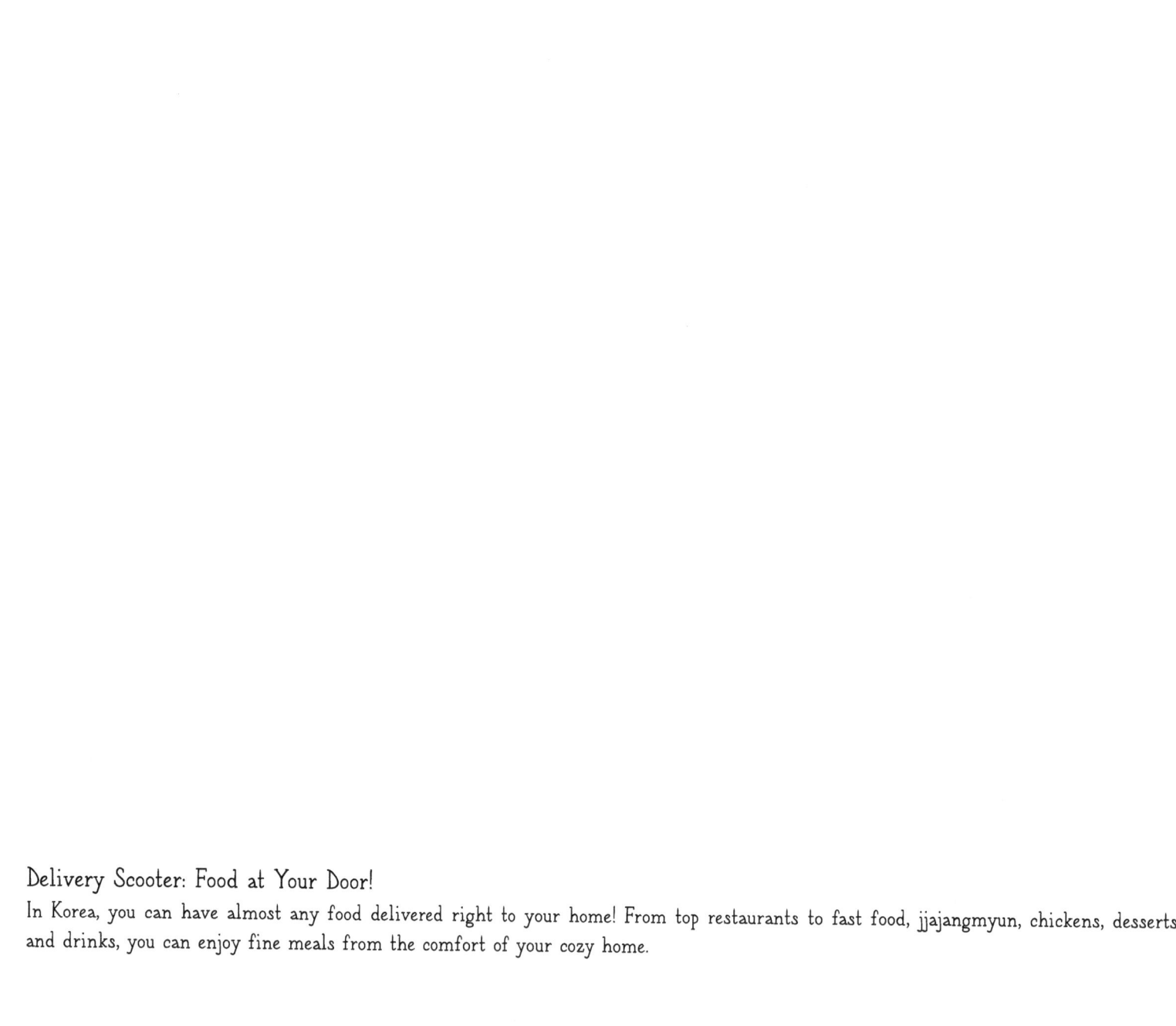

Delivery Scooter: Food at Your Door!
In Korea, you can have almost any food delivered right to your home! From top restaurants to fast food, jjajangmyun, chickens, desserts, and drinks, you can enjoy fine meals from the comfort of your cozy home.

Samgyetang: A Summer Superfood!
Samgyetang, Korean Chicken Ginseng Soup, is a must-eat during hot summer days. Koreans enjoy this nourishing dish to restore energy and stay strong in the heat. It's the smart way to beat the summer!

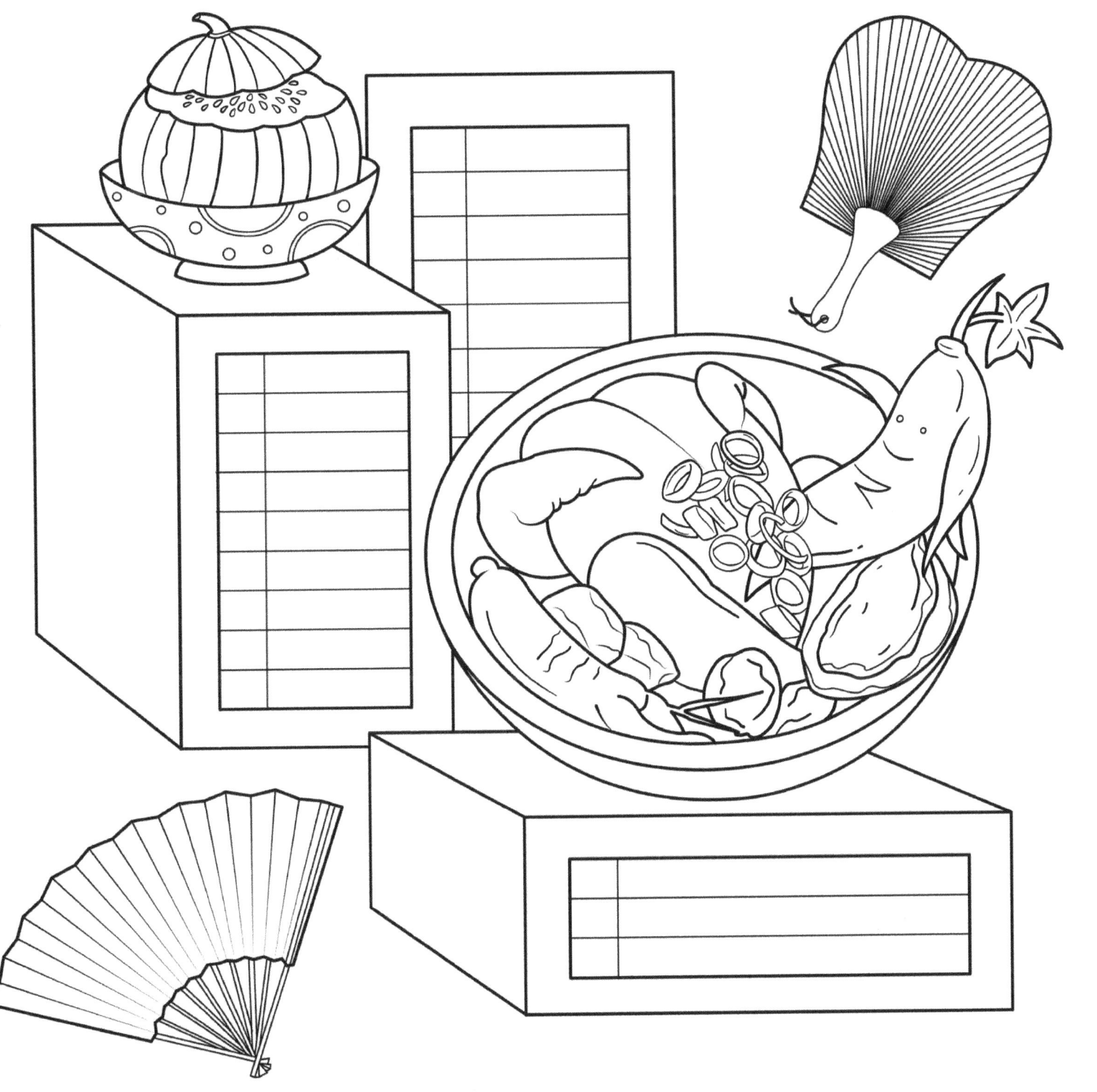

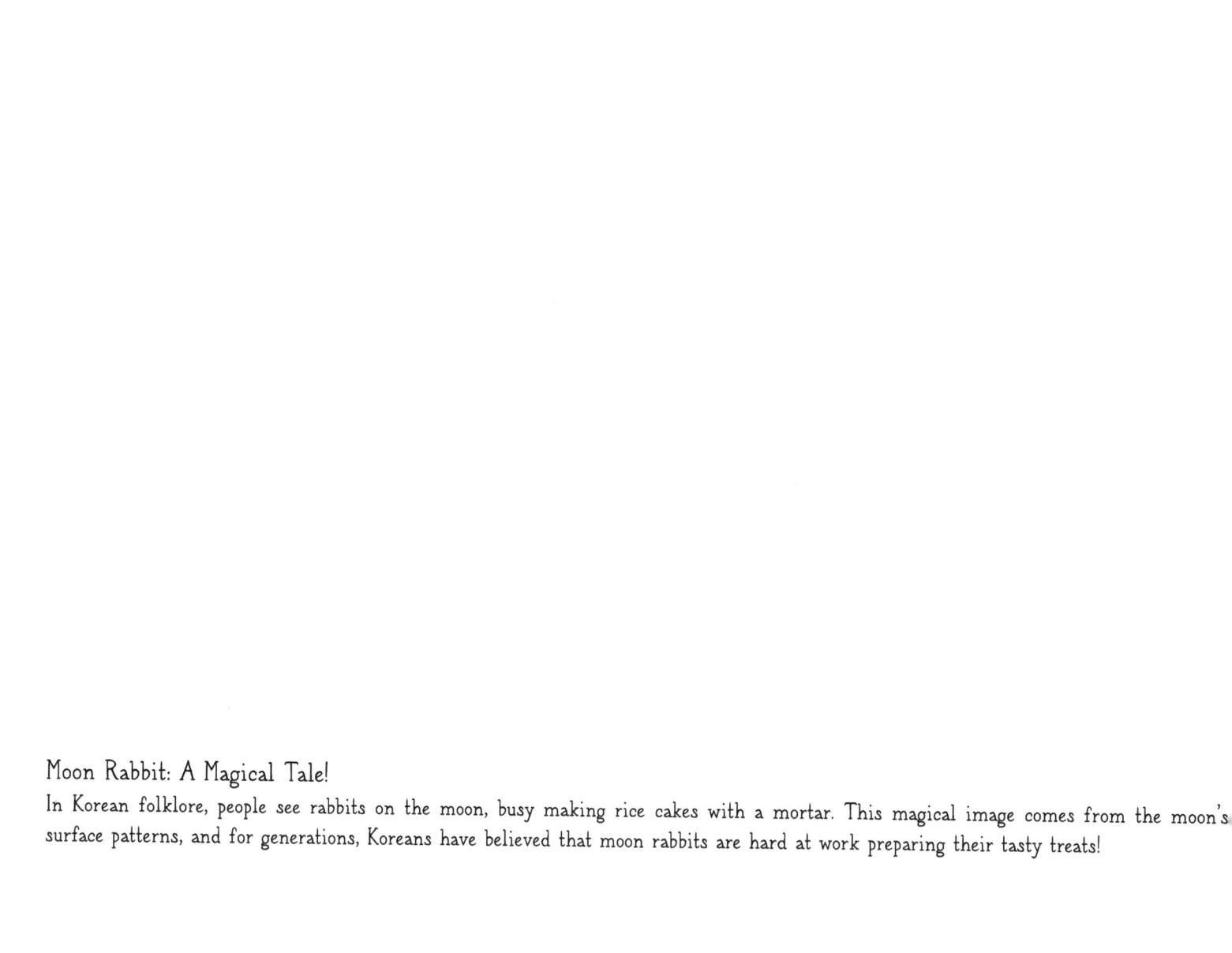

Moon Rabbit: A Magical Tale!

In Korean folklore, people see rabbits on the moon, busy making rice cakes with a mortar. This magical image comes from the moon's surface patterns, and for generations, Koreans have believed that moon rabbits are hard at work preparing their tasty treats!

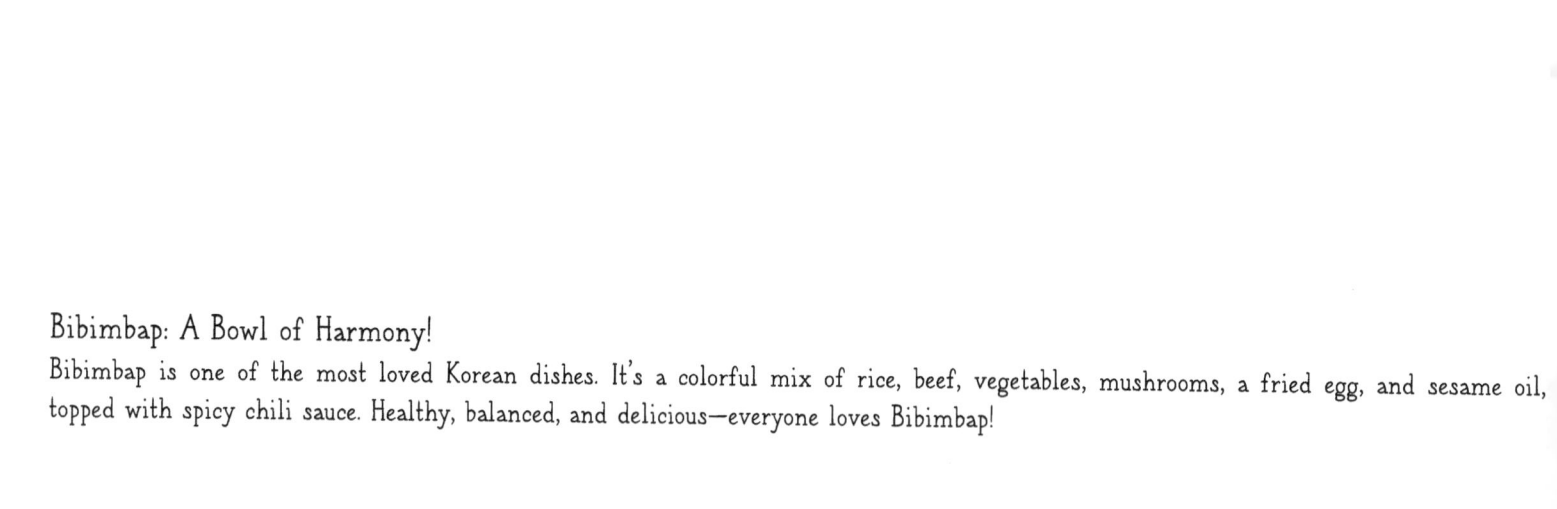

Bibimbap: A Bowl of Harmony!
Bibimbap is one of the most loved Korean dishes. It's a colorful mix of rice, beef, vegetables, mushrooms, a fried egg, and sesame oil, topped with spicy chili sauce. Healthy, balanced, and delicious—everyone loves Bibimbap!

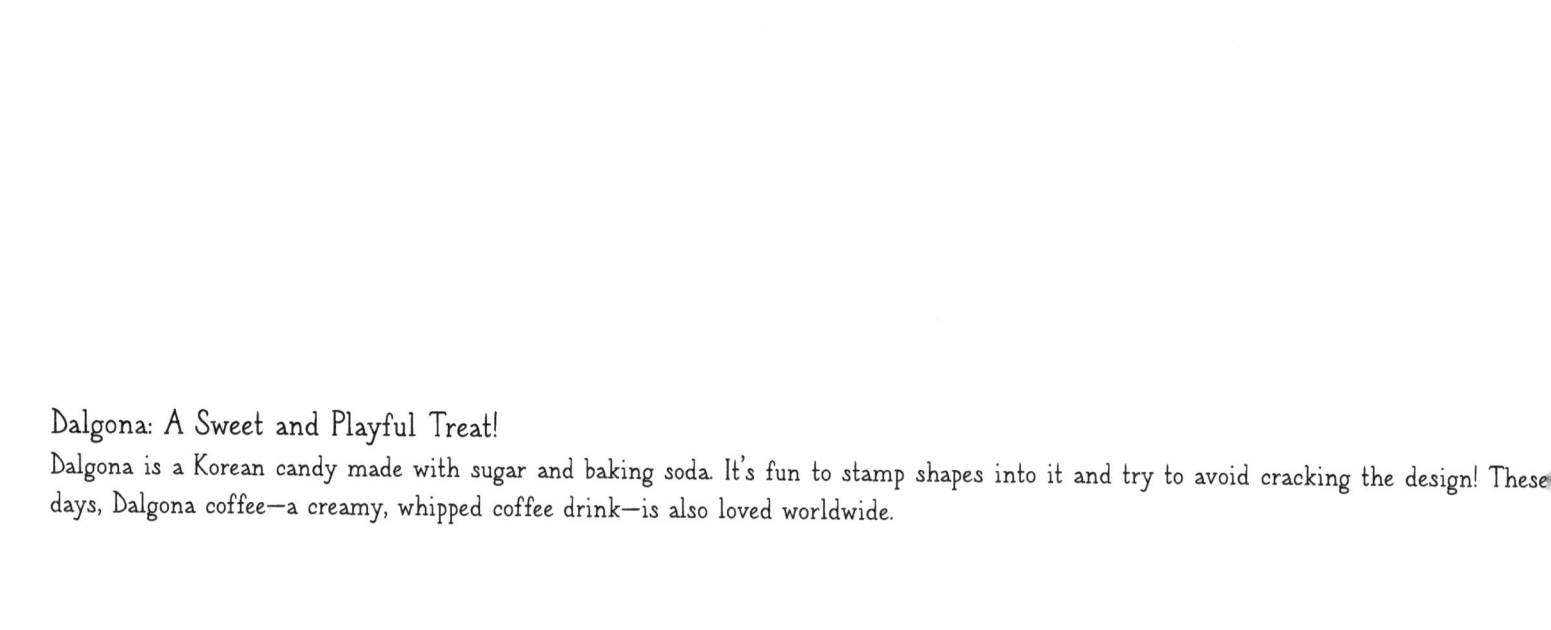

Dalgona: A Sweet and Playful Treat!

Dalgona is a Korean candy made with sugar and baking soda. It's fun to stamp shapes into it and try to avoid cracking the design! These days, Dalgona coffee—a creamy, whipped coffee drink—is also loved worldwide.

Korean Drinks: Cute and Tasty!
When you visit a Korean market, don't miss the drinks! From traditional sweet rice drinks to banana milk and coffee milk, they're not only delicious but come in the cutest designs!

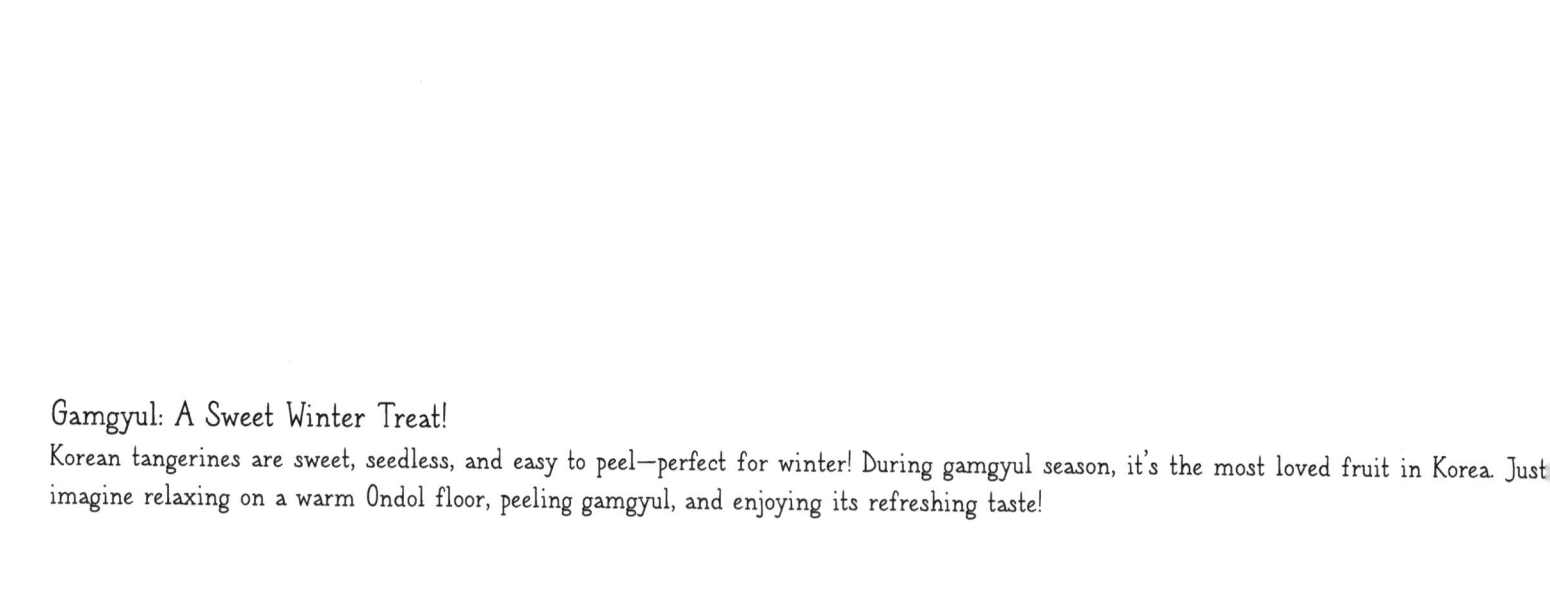

Gamgyul: A Sweet Winter Treat!

Korean tangerines are sweet, seedless, and easy to peel—perfect for winter! During gamgyul season, it's the most loved fruit in Korea. Just imagine relaxing on a warm Ondol floor, peeling gamgyul, and enjoying its refreshing taste!

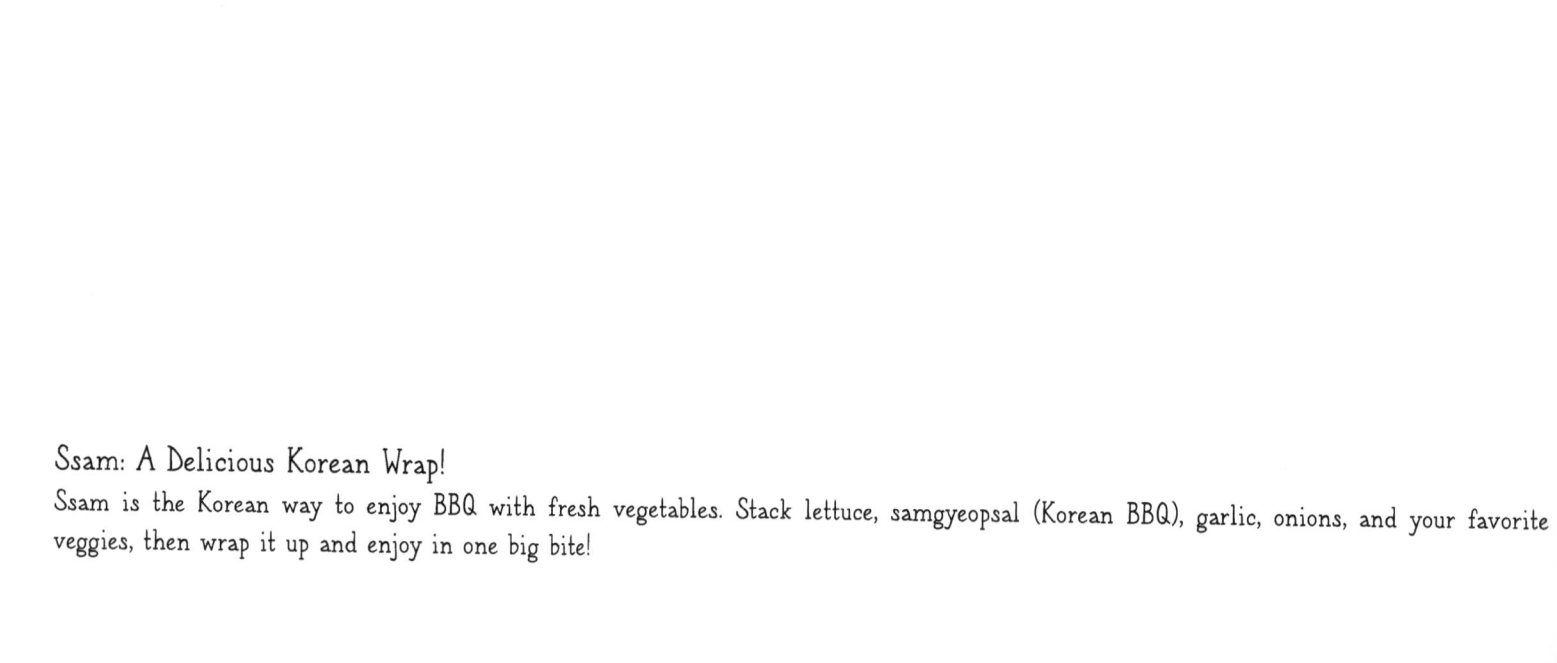

Ssam: A Delicious Korean Wrap!

Ssam is the Korean way to enjoy BBQ with fresh vegetables. Stack lettuce, samgyeopsal (Korean BBQ), garlic, onions, and your favorite veggies, then wrap it up and enjoy in one big bite!

Korean Convenience Stores: Always Open, Always Tasty!

In Korea, 24-hour convenience stores are everywhere, offering everything you need. From popular street food to ready-to-eat meals, you can grab delicious snacks anytime, day or night

Chocolate Pie Stacks: A Sweet Celebration!

In Korea, chocolate pies are a fun and easy way to make a birthday cake. Simple, rich, and delicious, these chocolate pie stacks are a quick and affordable way to celebrate the Korean way!

Korean Ice Cream: A Cool Surprise!
In Korea, you don't need an ice cream truck—just visit any nearby supermarket! From sherbet to ice cream cones, shark-shaped treats to watermelon flavors, Korean ice cream is full of fun and unexpected delights.

Mandu: A Delicious Korean Dumpling!
Mandu are dumplings stuffed with meat, vegetables, or even shrimp. With so many shapes and fillings to choose from, you can pick your favorite and enjoy this tasty Korean treat!

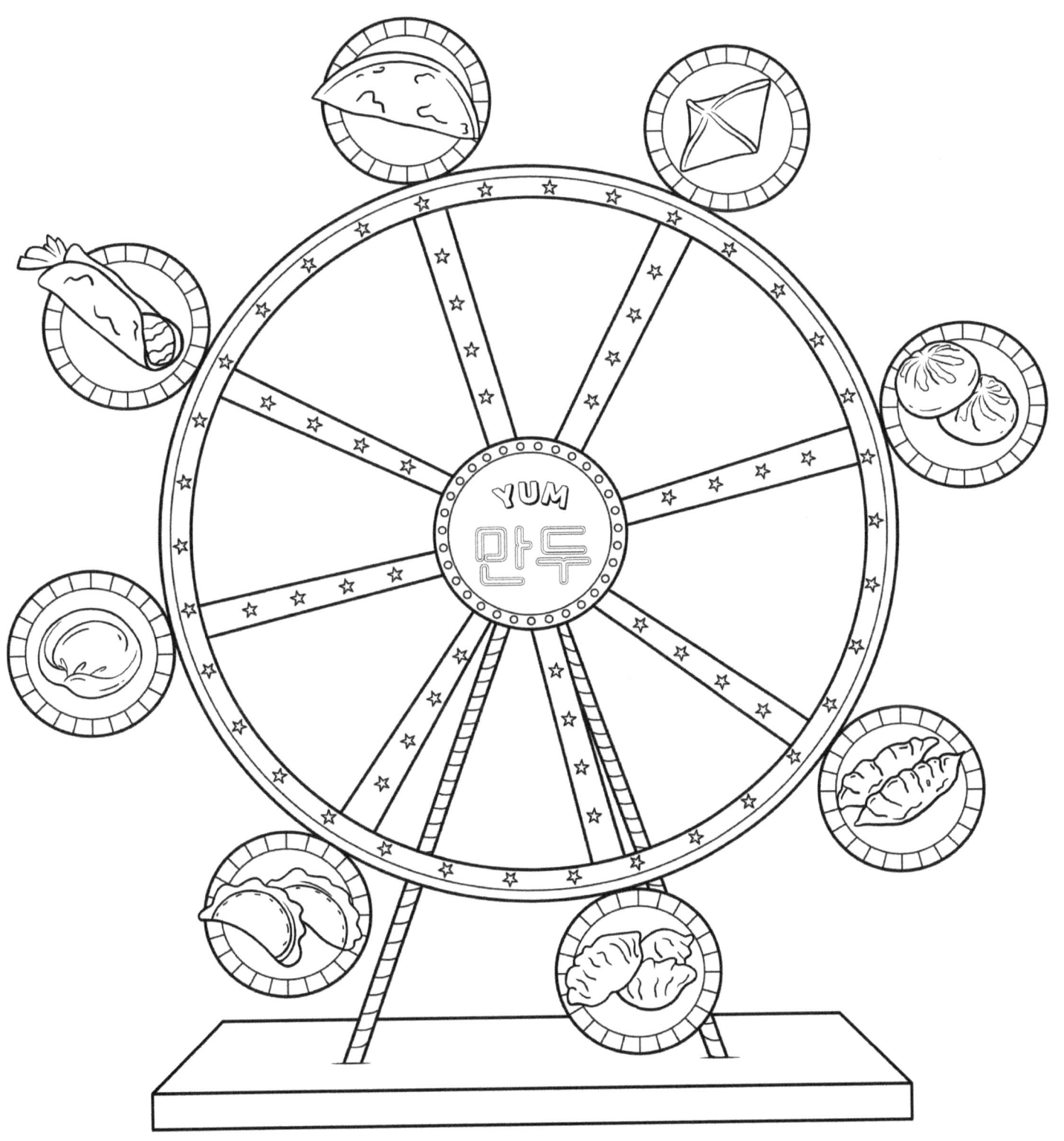

Winter Snacks: A Warm Winter Treat!

In winter, Korean streets are filled with the delicious smell of warm snacks. Stuffed with red beans, nuts, or sweet cream, these treats come in fun shapes like fish, flowers, and peanuts, making them as cute as they are tasty!

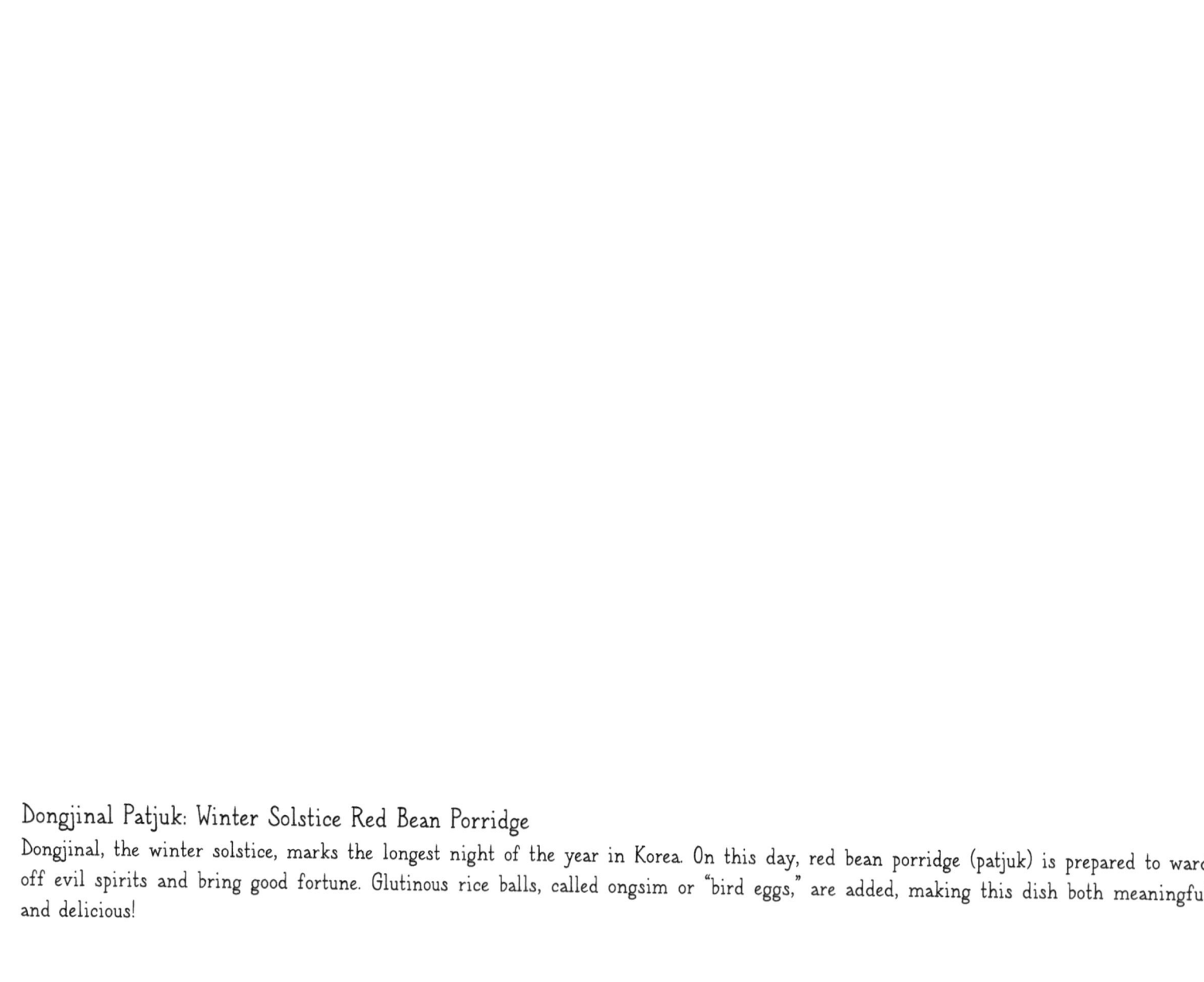

Dongjinal Patjuk: Winter Solstice Red Bean Porridge

Dongjinal, the winter solstice, marks the longest night of the year in Korea. On this day, red bean porridge (patjuk) is prepared to ward off evil spirits and bring good fortune. Glutinous rice balls, called ongsim or "bird eggs," are added, making this dish both meaningful and delicious!

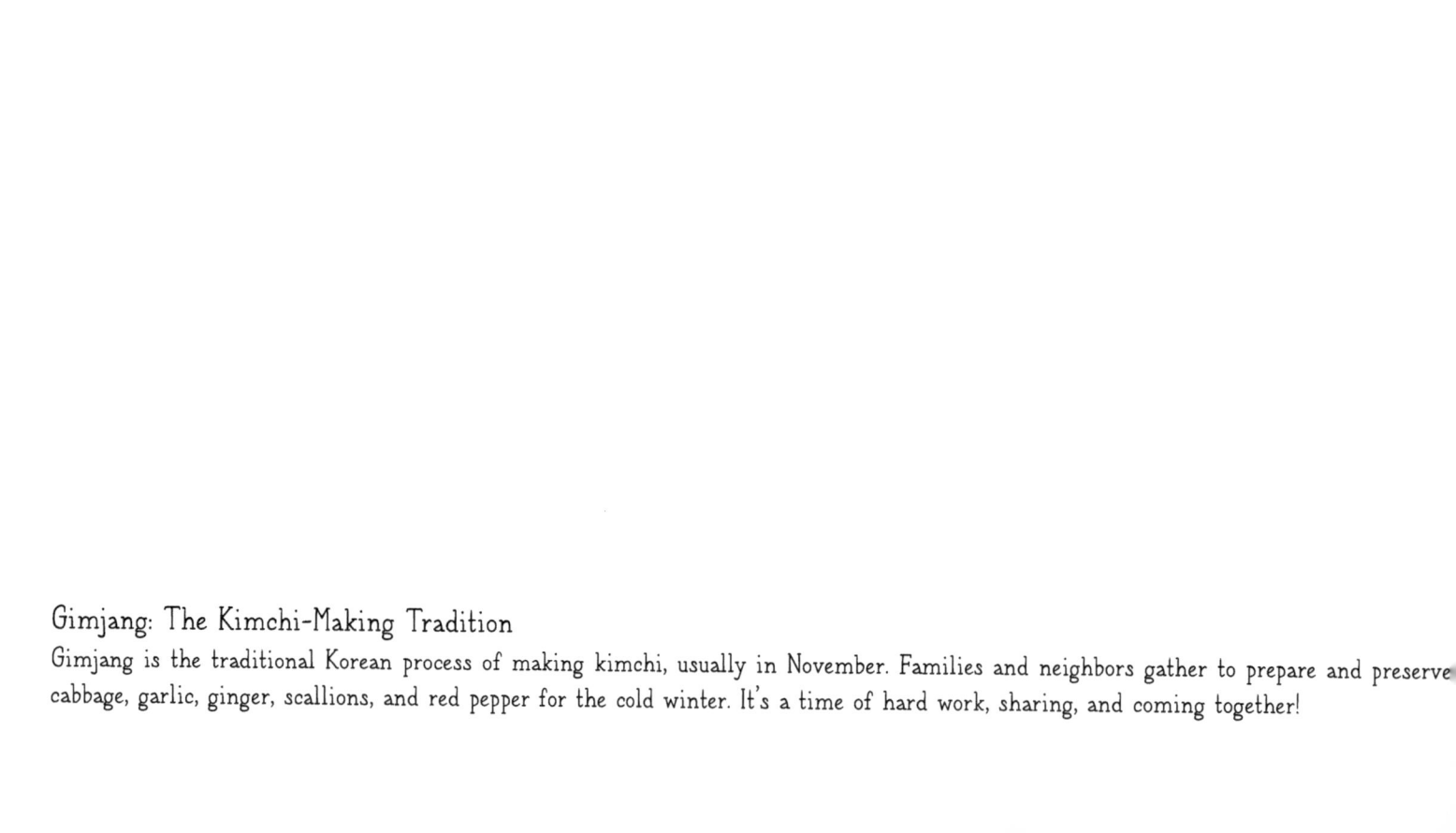

Gimjang: The Kimchi-Making Tradition

Gimjang is the traditional Korean process of making kimchi, usually in November. Families and neighbors gather to prepare and preserve cabbage, garlic, ginger, scallions, and red pepper for the cold winter. It's a time of hard work, sharing, and coming together!

Naengmyeon: Cold Noodles for Any Season!
Naengmyeon, literally "cold noodles," is a dish Koreans enjoy in both hot summers and chilly winters. Made with thin, chewy noodles of buckwheat and starch, it's a refreshing and unique way to embrace every season!

Korean Tea Ceremony: A Moment of Calm

The Korean tea ceremony is a mindful practice that brings calm and peace through the slow, careful process of making tea. From flower tea to leaf tea, and even cold ginger and cinnamon tea, it's a time to relax and enjoy. Tea is often served with delicate desserts, making it a soothing experience for both body and mind.

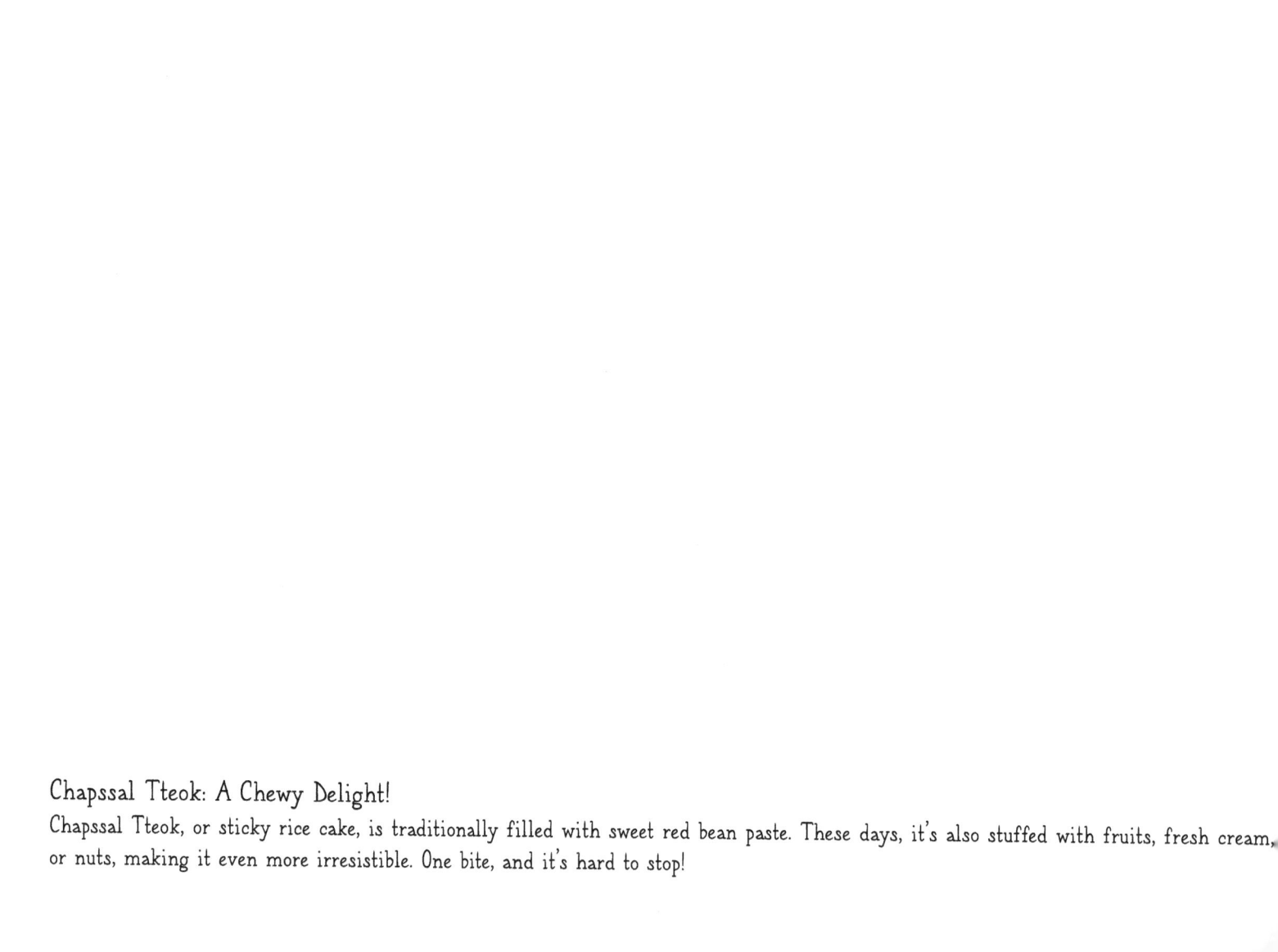

Chapssal Tteok: A Chewy Delight!

Chapssal Tteok, or sticky rice cake, is traditionally filled with sweet red bean paste. These days, it's also stuffed with fruits, fresh cream, or nuts, making it even more irresistible. One bite, and it's hard to stop!

Buchimgae: A Korean Savory Pancake

Buchimgae, or Korean pancakes, are a beloved dish in Korea, enjoyed as a light snack or a meal. They come in many varieties, like kimchi, seafood, zucchini, and mushrooms, offering something tasty for everyone

Buchimgae: A Korean Savory Pancake

Buchimgae, or Korean pancakes, are a beloved dish in Korea, enjoyed as a light snack or a meal. They come in many varieties, like kimchi, seafood, zucchini, and mushrooms, offering something tasty for everyone